ACKNOWLEDGEMENTS

This book is a labour of love, a tribute to the resilience, creativity, and spirit of India's street vendors. I extend our heartfelt gratitude to all those who have contributed to the creation of this visual journey celebrating the lives and livelihoods of these unsung heroes.

First and foremost, I'd like to express our deepest appreciation to the street vendors themselves, whose stories, talents, and perseverance have inspired every page of this book. Your dedication to your craft and your unwavering spirit in the face of challenges serve as a beacon of hope and resilience for us all. From bustling marketplaces to quiet alleyways, your willingness to open your hearts and share your stories has enriched this project immeasurably.

I'm also grateful to my friends, family, and mentor for their unwavering support and encouragement throughout the journey of creating this book. Your belief in my vision and your words of encouragement have been a source of strength and inspiration.

Last but not least, I'd like to thank the readers of "Bharat Bazaar" for embarking on this journey with me. May this book serve as a tribute to the indomitable spirit of India's street vendors and a reminder of the rich tapestry of culture, tradition, and resilience that thrives in every corner of our country.

DISCLAIMER

It is essential to recognize that the experiences of street vendors vary widely across different regions, communities, and socio-economic contexts. The portrayal of individuals and their livelihoods in this book is intended to provide a broad overview of the diverse landscape of Indian street markets, rather than an exhaustive depiction of every individual vendor's experience. Additionally, while efforts have been made to respect the privacy and dignity of the individuals featured in this book, some names, locations, and identifying details may have been altered or omitted to protect the privacy and confidentiality of the subjects.

The views, opinions, and perspectives expressed in this book belong solely to the authors and contributors and do not necessarily reflect the views or opinions of any organisations, institutions, or individuals mentioned herein.

Readers are encouraged to approach the content with respect, sensitivity, and a critical understanding of the complexities inherent in documenting the lives of others.

FOREWORD

In the bustling streets of India, amidst the cacophony of honking horns and bustling crowds, there exists a world unto itself—a world where the spirit of entrepreneurship thrives, and the rhythm of life beats to the pulse of the marketplace. It is a world inhabited by unsung heroes, whose stories are as diverse and colourful as the wares they sell. From the chaiwalas who brew their magic in tiny kettles to the nimble-fingered artisans who weave dreams with their hands, the streets of India are alive with the energy and resilience of its street vendors.

In "Bharat Bazaar," we embark on a journey through this vibrant tapestry of life, celebrating the lives and livelihoods of India's street vendors. Through captivating narratives and stunning visuals, this book offers a glimpse into the rich cultural heritage and entrepreneurial spirit that define India's street markets. This book is a testament to the power of community, creativity, and human connection. It is a reminder that amidst the hustle and bustle of modern life, there are pockets of humanity where traditions are preserved, dreams are nurtured, and bonds are forged.

Through this book, we hope to shine a spotlight on the often-overlooked contributions of India's street vendors to the fabric of our society. We invite you to join us on this journey of discovery, as we celebrate the resilience, creativity, and spirit of India's unsung heroes.

INTRODUCTION

THE CULTURE OF STREET MARKETS IN INDIA

India's diversity hosts a vibrant variety of street markets that are not just spaces of commerce, but also repositories of culture, history, and community. This tradition of selling can be traced back centuries, where caravans traversed cities selling goods, often exchanging them with other things that could be potentially of use elsewhere. With the advent of time and the organic evolution of religions, dynasties, and cities, this barter system soon made headway for an exchange of currency, embodying the spirit of entrepreneurship that define it as we know today. In a culturally diverse country like India, each region boasts of its own unique marketplaces—the spice-scented lanes of Khari Baoli in Delhi, the textile emporiums of Kanchipuram, or even the antique stalls in Kolkata—that provide a livelihood to millions of artisans, traders, and small-scale entrepreneurs.

The low entry barriers and direct access to customers make them an incubator for grassroot businesses, and thus the hubs of the country's informal sector that contribute to around 7% of the GDP of India. They also generate a multitude of employment opportunities: suppliers, distributors, transporters, and support services that are open to marginalised communities, migrants, and the urban poor. Moreover, they serve as attractions for tourists—domestic and international—offering immersive experiences that are opportunities for cultural exchange and contribute directly to the local economy. Meanwhile, the popularity of these markets through exports contributes to foreign exchange earnings and enhances India's global economic presence.

Additionally, they also play a critical role in safeguarding the country's heritage. Many artisans, craftsmen and traditional vendors ply their trade in street markets, passing down age-old techniques and craftsmanship from one generation to the next. By providing a platform for these artisans to showcase their skills while also evolving to the latest trends, street markets thus foster an appreciation for India's indigenous crafts amongst consumers and bolster the resilience of local economies.

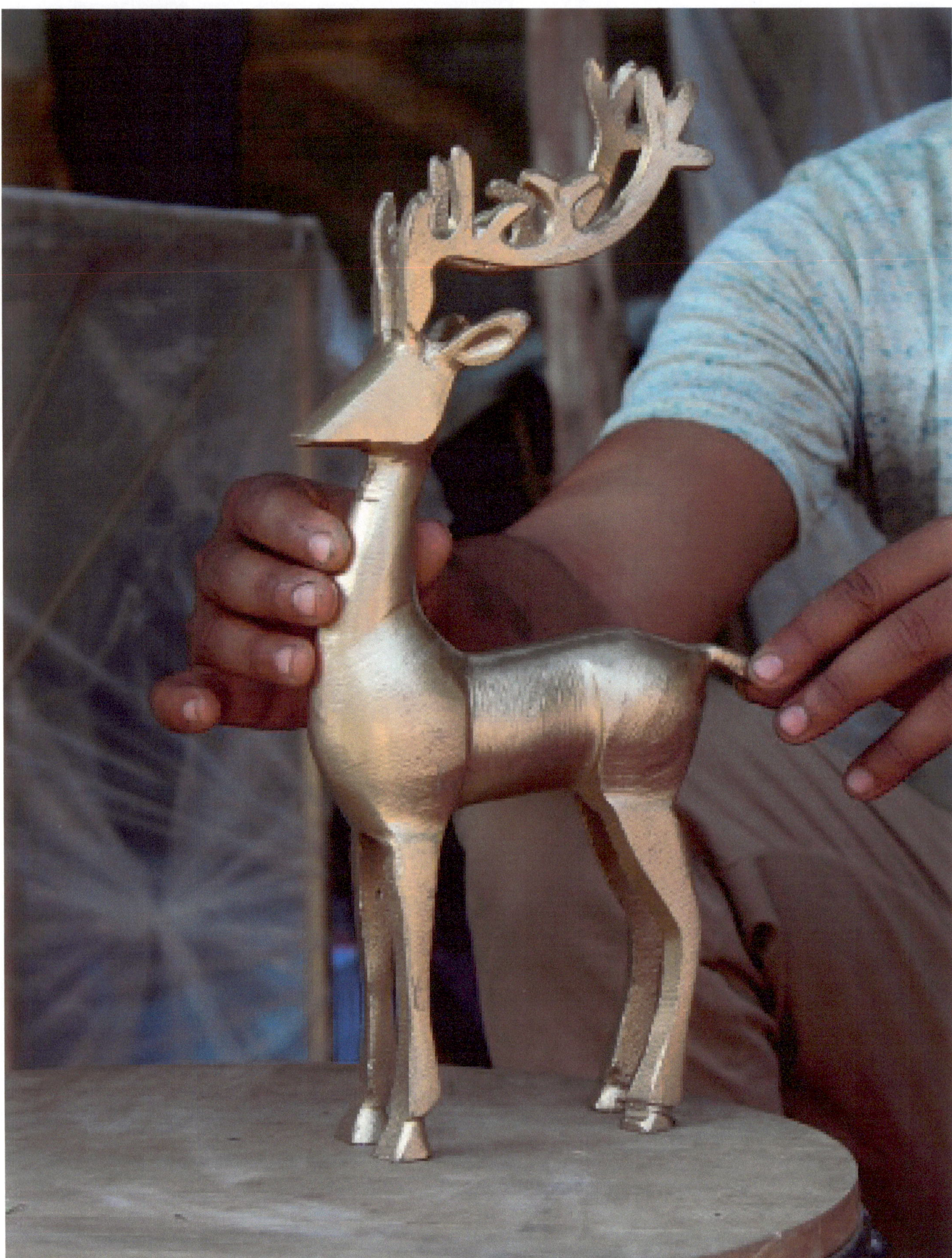

CHALLENGES

In the realm of hand-crafted goods, a complex tapestry unfolds, where potters, lamp sellers, glass cutters, furniture makers, and mosaic artists intersect, each bringing their unparalleled skill, passion, and creativity to their craft. In the realm of hand-crafted goods, a complex tapestry unfolds, where potters, lamp sellers, glass cutters, furniture makers, and mosaic artists intersect, each bringing their unparalleled skill, passion, and creativity to their craft.

Additionally, alternative income streams present an unpleasant truth - sales fluctuate greatly, resulting in inconsistent incomes and heightened financial insecurity. Furthermore, the lack of appreciation for their talent poses another significant challenge. They are often seen as vendors rather than artists, undermining their professional dignity and exacerbating their difficulties. And if these challenges were not enough, bureaucracy further compounds their struggles. Furthermore, the lack of appreciation for their talent poses another significant challenge. They are often seen as vendors rather than artists, undermining their professional dignity and exacerbating their difficulties. And if these challenges were not enough, bureaucracy further compounds their struggles. Nevertheless, despite the multitude of obstacles that stand in the way of success, these craftsmen persevere, displaying resilience through their brushstrokes and kiln-fired creations. In their hands, they hold not only the tools of their trade but also the dreams and aspirations of a vibrant community of artisans, united by their passion for their craft and their unwavering determination to overcome any challenges that may come their way.

The process of modernization and technology has made conventional crafts appear as old fashioned and unprofitable professions. This change not only puts at risk rich cultural heritage but also lives of skilled craftsmen who depend on the trade for their living. Furthermore, no apprenticeship programs or formal education exist in most traditional craft areas. These factors make it hard for them to pass down their knowledge to the next generation. To overcome these obstacles, promoting an understanding of traditional crafts is essential, assistance in developing skills is important and there must be ways through which younger people can interact with and appreciate evergreen art forms.

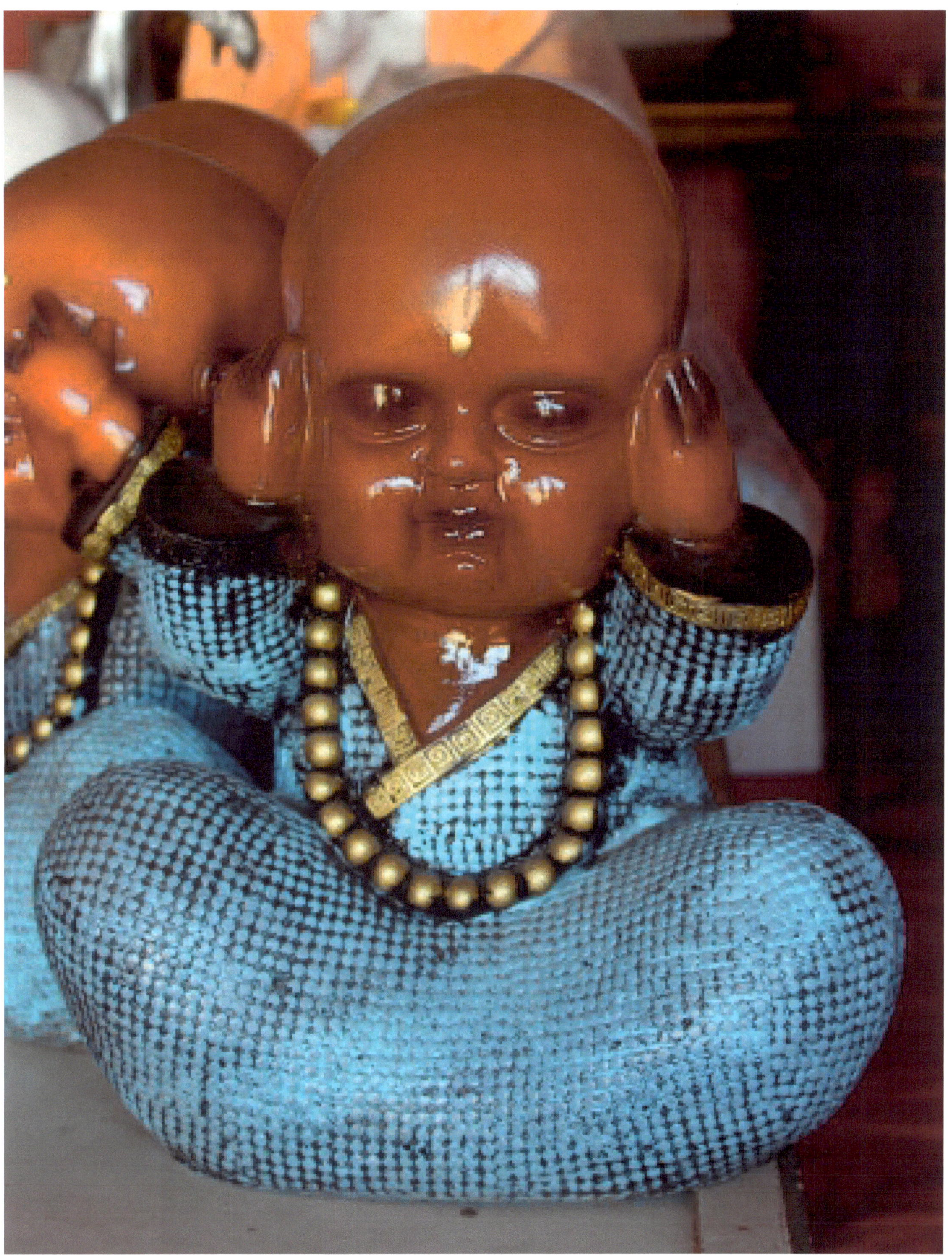

WHAT CAN WE DO TO HELP THEM?

India's cities are teeming with intricately designed streets and bustling squares, resonating with the calls of street vendors. Each vendor has a story of resilience - from those hawking on every street corner to nimble-fingered craftsmen assembling vibrant trinkets. However, there is more to these individuals than meets the eye, and amidst the clamor, a lingering question remains: "How can we help?" And the simplest answer is of course to buy local and support these artisans. Additionally, by advocating for regulations that foster fair competition, everyone can benefit from a level playing field. Through educational initiatives, these artisans gain the skills required for upward mobility while directly supporting their businesses. This effort to highlight the beauty and resilience in such a staple aspect of Indian life hopes to not only fill stomachs but also nurture dreams. One must accord the dignity of the artist to the vendor as well.

CONCLUSION

As India strides towards a digital future, amidst a whirlwind of progress and modernization, it is crucial to not overlook the artisans and craftsmen who form the backbone of our cultural heritage. The bustling streets and vibrant markets form the backbone of our cultural heritage, and their stories of resilience and creativity are integral to the fabric of our society. In our quest for modernity, we musn't forget their contributions to the foundation of our heritage, and we must enable them to thrive in a rapidly changing world.

In our role as consumers, we wield significant power to make a tangible difference in the lives of local artisans and craftsmen. By choosing to prioritise locally made products and supporting businesses that prioritise ethical practices, we can directly impact the livelihoods of artisans and contribute to the preservation of traditional craftsmanship. Every purchase we make is a vote for the kind of world we want to live in. When we opt for handmade goods over mass-produced items, we signal our appreciation for the time, skill, and cultural heritage embedded in each piece. Moreover, by consciously seeking out and patronising street markets and artisanal collectives, we create demand for authentic, handcrafted products, thereby incentivizing artisans to continue practising their craft.